M000159804

Breathe

A CHILD'S GUIDE TO ASCENSION, PENTECOST, AND THE GROWING TIME

Laura Alary
Illustrated by Cathrin Peterslund

PARACLETE PRESS
BREWSTER, MASSACHUSETTS

2021 First Printing

Breathe: A Child's Guide to Ascension, Pentecost, and the Growing Time

Text copyright © 2021 by Laura Alary

ISBN 978-1-64060-560-2

The Paraclete Press name and logo (dove on cross) are trademarks of Paraclete Press.

Library of Congress Cataloging-in-Publication Data

Names: Alary, Laura, author. | Peterslund, Cathrin, 1991- illustrator.
Title: Breathe : a child's guide to Ascension, Pentecost, and the growing
    time / Laura Alary ; illustrated by Cathrin Peterslund.
Description: Brewster, Massachusetts : Paraclete Press, 2021. | Summary:
    "The Biblical movements of Jesus and the Spirit are explored and
    interwoven with contemporary reflections from the view of a child"–
    Provided by publisher.
Identifiers: LCCN 2020042094 (print) | LCCN 2020042095 (ebook) | ISBN
    9781640605602 (trade paperback) | ISBN 9781640605619 (epub) | ISBN
    9781640605626 (pdf)
Subjects: LCSH: Pentecost season–Juvenile literature. | Jesus
    Christ–Ascension–Juvenile literature. | Children–Religious
    life–Juvenile literature.
Classification: LCC BV61 .A43 2021 (print) | LCC BV61 (ebook) | DDC
    242/.62–dc23
LC record available at https://lccn.loc.gov/2020042094
LC ebook record available at https://lccn.loc.gov/2020042095

10 9 8 7 6 5 4 3 2 1

All rights reserved. No portion of this book may be reproduced,
stored in an electronic retrieval system, or transmitted in any form or
by any means—electronic, mechanical, photocopy, recording, or any
other—except for brief quotations in printed reviews, without the prior
permission of the publisher.

Published by Paraclete Press
Brewster, Massachusetts
www.paracletepress.com

Manufactured by PRINPIA Co., Ltd.
54, Gasanro 9-Gil, Geumcheon-gu, Seoul 08513, Korea
Printed in January 2021, Seoul, South Korea

For Claire, through whom the Spirit flows and breathes
and changes the world.

The day of Pentecost is coming.
The church is changing color.
The white and gold of Easter
will soon burst into flaming red,
then cool to green.

The world outside has its own seasons.
It is changing colors, too.

In many places, the whites and browns of winter
have been folded away for another year.
Colors are bursting out everywhere—
wildflowers in ditches,
birds flashing bright wings,
dandelions popping out in unexpected places.

Everything is greening.

It feels like the sleeping world
is waking up again.
Taking a deep breath, getting ready to grow.

Breathless

The news left them breathless.

"I am going away," said Jesus.
"You will not see me anymore."

His friends could not understand.
On that terrible day when Jesus died
their world seemed to crumble.
They held tight to one another
to keep from tumbling into emptiness.

But then—how was it possible?
*   —he was back!*

Wild joy sprang up in them.
This time, they promised,
we will hold onto him and
*   never let go.*

But Jesus shattered their hopes.
Like small children, his friends
*   clung to him,*
overflowing with questions:

"Where are you going?"
"Can we come too?"
"When will you come back?"
"Who will stay with us?"

But Jesus gathered them close,
*   and said:*

"Don't be afraid.
I will never leave you alone.
A helper is coming
*   to show you the way.*
To stand by you.
To comfort you.
To be with you always.
Wait and watch."

Then he was gone, like smoke from
*   a candle, dissolving into thin air.*

They held their breath and waited.

Sometimes I hold my breath
when I am scared
or when something hurts a lot.
Saying goodbye to someone you love hurts.
When they go they leave an empty space
no one else can fill.
Other people come, but it is not the same.

I wonder why Jesus came back to his friends,
only to go away again.
Why did he get their hopes up?
That must have hurt.
They must have been afraid.

I guess everyone is afraid sometimes.

Afraid of losing someone important.

Afraid of new things.

Afraid of change.

Afraid of being alone.

It would help to have a friend who never goes away.

I wonder who that could be?

On the last Sunday of Easter
We hear the story of the Ascension.
That is a big word that means *going up*.
As we hear the story of how Jesus went back to God,
the storyteller lights a candle,
then puts out the flame.
A curlicue of smoke rises,
then dissolves into the air.

I can smell it even after it disappears.
The light is still with us in some way.
But it is not the same.

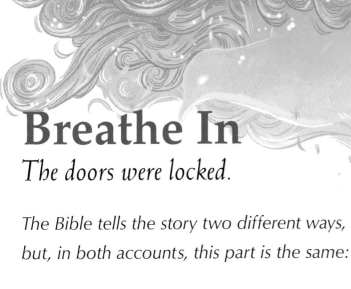

Breathe In
The doors were locked.

The Bible tells the story two different ways,
but, in both accounts, this part is the same:

After Jesus went away,
his friends huddled together
behind thick walls and locked doors.
Fear squeezed their throats
until it was hard to breathe.
They had no idea what they
were waiting for,
but Jesus had promised.
A helper was coming.

Then the story splits in two,
like branches of a tree.

In one branch the Spirit comes like fire,
showering everyone with sparks,
until their fear is burned away,

and they crackle with courage
to say and do new things—
things they never thought
they could.
Unruly as a wild wind,
the Spirit scatters them like seeds.
Wherever they settle
they tell the story of Jesus
in different ways,
so everyone can understand.

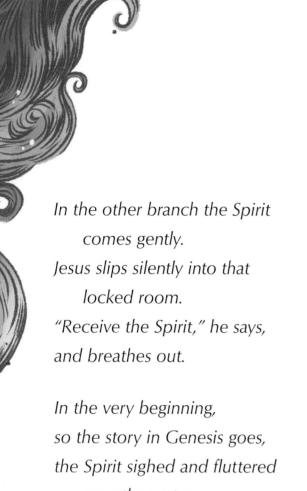

In the other branch the Spirit
   comes gently.
Jesus slips silently into that
   locked room.
"Receive the Spirit," he says,
and breathes out.

In the very beginning,
so the story in Genesis goes,
the Spirit sighed and fluttered
   over the waters,
breathing life into the world.

As they sit quietly with Jesus,
breathing in,
his friends feel their hearts
settle into a steady beat.
Their fear drains away, and they
   feel alive again.

Jesus slips away unnoticed,
but his friends are no longer afraid.
Now they understand.
The Spirit that was in Jesus is in
   them too.
Always.
As close as their own breath.

On the day of Pentecost
the church is dressed in red—the color of fire.
We celebrate the gift of the Spirit with a cake and candles,
streamers and pinwheels.
The wind catches them and sets them spinning.
It breathes into the banners over our heads
and makes them dance.

I can't see the wind, but I know
     when it is near.
It makes things move.

13

On the night of Pentecost, we have a bonfire.
The blaze makes a circle of warmth.
It lights up our faces as we sing.
A spark leaps out and burns a hole in my blanket.

Maybe anything powerful can
destroy as well as create.
Maybe they go together, like death and life.

PEACE JOY LOVE HOPE

I am learning new ways to pray
with the wind and my own breath.

Some days I blow bubbles
and watch the breeze carry them.
Each bubble is a prayer for someone.

We use scissors, fabric, and glue
to make prayer flags.
I put words on mine:
Peace. Hope. Love. Joy. Welcome.
We hang them outside.

When the wind passes by it makes
them flutter.

I wonder who will see my prayers.
I wonder how far my prayers can go.

WELCOME

I like to lie on my back in the grass on a warm day,
watching the clouds.
I imagine my breath is making them move.
In and out. In and out.
My belly rises and falls as the clouds drift across the sky.

Sometimes I add a few words:

Peace.   **_Jesus._**   **_Thank you._**   **_Spirit._**   **_Breathe in me._**

I like to run and jump and move,
but I notice a lot more when I just sit.
Sometimes it is good to be still.

I feel like I am getting ready for something.
I wonder what the Spirit will do through me.

Breathe Out

When they felt the Spirit in them,
connecting them with Jesus,
his friends began to say and do
the things Jesus had done.

They healed.
They welcomed strangers.
They shared what they had.

They listened and understood.
They forgave.
They loved with open hearts.

The Spirit flowed through them,
breathed through them,
changed the world through them,
sometimes in surprising ways.

Ananias and Saul were both surprised by the Spirit.
Ananias was a follower of Jesus,
Saul dead set against him.
Ananias was open-hearted and wide-eyed,
always seeing sameness beneath differences.
Saul was sharp-minded,
with a keen eye for opposites:
Good. Bad. Right. Wrong. Inside. Outside. Us. Them.
Saul saw Ananias and his sort
as a threat to God's ordered world.
So he set out to hunt them down.

When Ananias heard Saul was coming
he locked the doors and held his breath.
But when have locked doors ever stopped the Spirit?
When those doors were blown wide open,
Ananias gave up trying to hide
    and went searching for Saul.

But the Spirit found Saul first. Ambushed him.
Knocked him flat. Made him see stars. The Spirit said:

    "Why are you doing this?
    What are you afraid of?"

Maybe they were both afraid:
Saul, breathless and blind,
at the mercy of the one he had wanted to destroy.
Ananias, still wary, but trying to love his enemy.

In the end, love proved stronger than fear.
Ananias brought Saul into his own home,
looked after him,
listened to his story,
tried to understand him.
Even his name changed: Saul became Paul.

And when his eyes were finally opened,
Paul looked at Ananias and saw a friend.
Paul was changed in more ways than one.

Many years later,
Paul wrote to some friends about how you know
when the Spirit is at work:

Picture a tree. Its roots drink water from the ground.
Sunlight falls on its leaves.
The wind carries pollen from blossom to blossom.
Soon the branches are heavy with sweet fruit.
Then you know the tree is full of life.

It is the same with you.
    When the Spirit is in you,
you can see the good things that grow:
Kindness. Patience. Gentleness. Goodness.
Faithfulness. Self-Control. Peace. Joy. Love.
These are the fruits of the Spirit.

Maybe Paul was remembering
        Ananias
and the sweet taste of kindness.

The season after Pentecost lasts for a long time—
over half the circle of the year.
In church we call it Ordinary Time.
I'm not sure why.

There are no big holidays during Ordinary Time,
but life in the Spirit is not ordinary.
Amazing things are happening.

The seeds we planted in the spring are waking up.
Beans are popping out of the soil.
Flowers are blooming.
In the pond close by, tadpoles are becoming frogs.

Everything is growing and changing.

We feed our garden with rich black earth
from the compost pile.
All through the winter we collected scraps:
vegetable peelings, eggshells, coffee grounds.

Stirring it was my job.
I never liked the wriggly worms or clouds of flies.
But I love how the bits and pieces we throw away
turn into something good,
something that makes our garden grow.

I wonder if even that is the Spirit at work.

One of my favorite parts of summer
is spending a week at a cottage near the ocean.
We walk on the beach, jump in the waves, and fly kites.
The wind makes me feel alive.
I fill my pockets with sea glass.
When I get home, I make pictures with the bits of glass.
I like how the sea and I
both make something beautiful from broken pieces.
Maybe the Spirit does that, too.

By mid-summer our garden is full of good things.

Almost too full.

There is more than we can use

so we share with our neighbors.

We bring baskets of carrots and beans

to our community food bank.

We make casseroles and freeze them.

If someone needs a meal, we are ready.

It feels good to know that the seeds we planted are bearing fruit.

Bees and butterflies visit our garden.

We chose plants they love:

Black-Eyed Susan. Echinacea. Bee Balm.

Without these tiny creatures

to pollinate our trees and plants,

we would have no flowers or fruit.

    Imagine a world without blueberry pie!

We need them. They need us.
   We are all connected.

We planted milkweed for the
   monarch butterflies.
These tiny travelers have a long
   journey south.
Our garden is a safe place
   where they can rest,
lay their eggs, and feed their
   families.

Butterflies are not the only ones that migrate.

People do, too.

Some choose to move. Others have no choice.

I try to imagine what it would be like to have to move.

What would I carry with me?

What would I leave behind?

What would I miss most?

I hope someone would make a safe place for me.

One hot day my friends and I sell homemade lemonade.

All the money we earn we give away

to help families looking for safe places to live.

We are far away but we can still help.

We need each other to do the work of Jesus.

The Spirit connects us all.

At our church camp
we make care packages
for people who live on the street
    or in shelters.
We decorate paper bags
and fill them with toothbrushes
    and toothpaste,
soap, shampoo, and socks.

At night as I brush my teeth
I notice the clean water,
my new toothbrush,
the lemony smell of the soap.

When I pay attention, I notice more.

The more I notice, the more
    grateful I am.

Maybe the Spirit is waking me up.
Maybe I am growing the fruits of
    kindness.

Time to Grow

Summer is turning to autumn.

I feel it in the cool evenings.

I see it in the clear blue skies and yellow goldenrod.

I hear it in the cries of geese heading south.

In our garden, pumpkins are green on the vine.

By next month they will be brushed with orange.

The milkweed is heavy with fat pods,

bursting at the seams with feathery seeds.

I wonder where the wind will carry them.

Before the new school year begins,

my church has another picnic.

There is fresh corn and lots of berry pies—

the sweet harvest of our gardens.

We also share bread and wine,
just like in church.
Someone reads the words of Jesus:

"I am the vine. You are the branches.
Remain in me and you will bring forth much fruit."

We also hear part of a letter from Paul.
I remember Paul—and how he got that name.

Paul says that when we share this meal,
we need to remember we are all one body—
the body of Christ.

When I taste the bread and wine,
I imagine that I am eating
everything that makes things grow:
Earth. Air. Sun. Rain.
The Spirit that gives life to everything is in me, too.

Around me I see the faces of my church family.
Some I have known my whole life. Others are new.
People come and go, but we are all connected—
to each other, and to Jesus.
We are all like cells in one body,
growing and changing, part of something bigger.

The same Spirit breathes in all of us.

I used to wonder how Jesus could go away,
and yet promise to be with us always.
Now I am starting to see.

The Spirit that was in Jesus is in us, too.
We are his body now,
his way of being in the world.

Whenever we choose kindness,
make peace,
live gently,
show patience,
feel joy,
give love,
Jesus is there.
Always.

The Spirit is like seeds,
and like the breath of the wind that carries them.

It is within us and beyond us.

I am part of this.
The Spirit is in me, too.

You are part of this.
The Spirit is in you, too.

I wonder what kind of fruit I will bring to the world.

This is the Growing Time.

You may also be interested in these by Laura Alary...

Make Room

A Child's Guide to Lent and Easter

Illustrated by Ann Boyajian

ISBN 978-1-61261-659-9

Trade paperback | $15.99

Look!

A Child's Guide to Advent and Christmas

Illustrated by Ann Boyajian

ISBN 978-1-61261-866-1

Trade paperback | $16.99

AVAILABLE AT BOOKSTORES

Paraclete Press | 1-800-451-5006 | www.paracletepress.com